Mandala Mayhem

True Coloring
Stress Relieving Mandalas

Shari Daniel

True Coloring is a group of artists, authors, and avid colorists from around the world. We share a passion for creativity, expression, and the therapeutic benefits of art in all its forms.

We all express ourselves differently and enjoy different themes, but we are joined by the goal of sharing our unique works with you in the hope you enjoy coloring as much as we have enjoyed creating.

We are dedicated to sharing our passion with you by providing affordable, quality coloring books for coloring enthusiasts of all skill levels in a wide selection of sizes and styles.

Coloring Tips

❖ Have your tool(s) of choice, from colored pastels to markers to color pencils to crayons to water colors to gel pens ready.

❖ If you like, you could play some soothing music to set the tone for coloring.

❖ Flip through this coloring book and see which of the mandalas appeal to you for the coloring activity of the day. Feel for something simple? There's sure to be a design that's perfect for you. Want a more challenging design? There's a complicated design right up your alley.

❖ Think about the colors you'll want to use. Do you want to just go with the flow and choose your colors at random? Or do you want to plan the colors you want to use? The choice is all up to you.

❖ After that, the next step is to sit back, take a few calming breaths and start coloring.

❖ When you're done, look at the mandala you've finished coloring. Do you feel it? The energy that emanates from it? I bet you do. You can keep it to yourself, but where you'll see it every single day, such as on the refrigerator door, or as a screen saver on your phone. On the other hand, you can share it with your friends, family and acquaintances, in person, or through your social media of choice. It's all up to you.

There isn't a right or wrong way to color; just use your creativity and have loads of fun!

ENJOY!

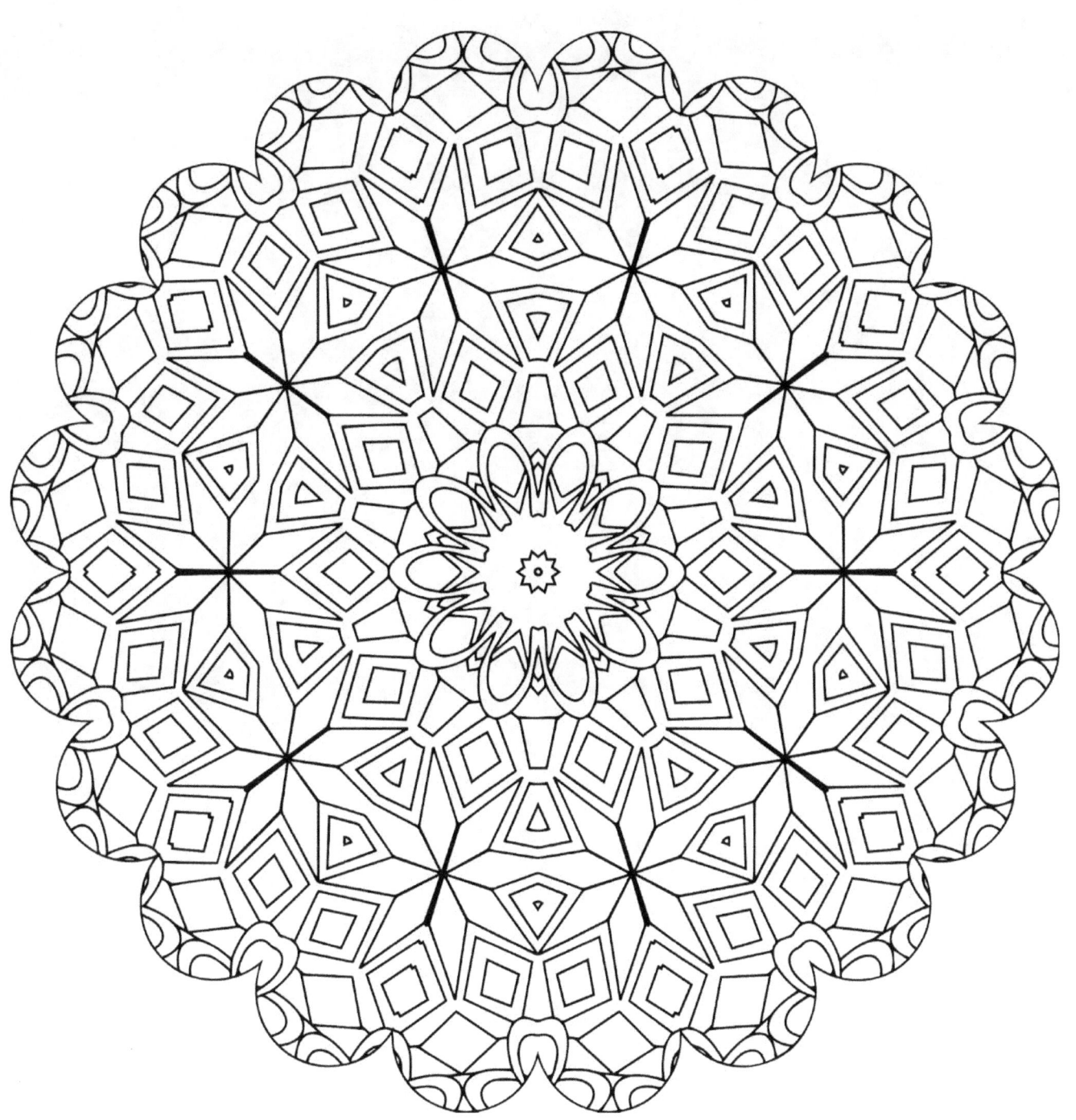

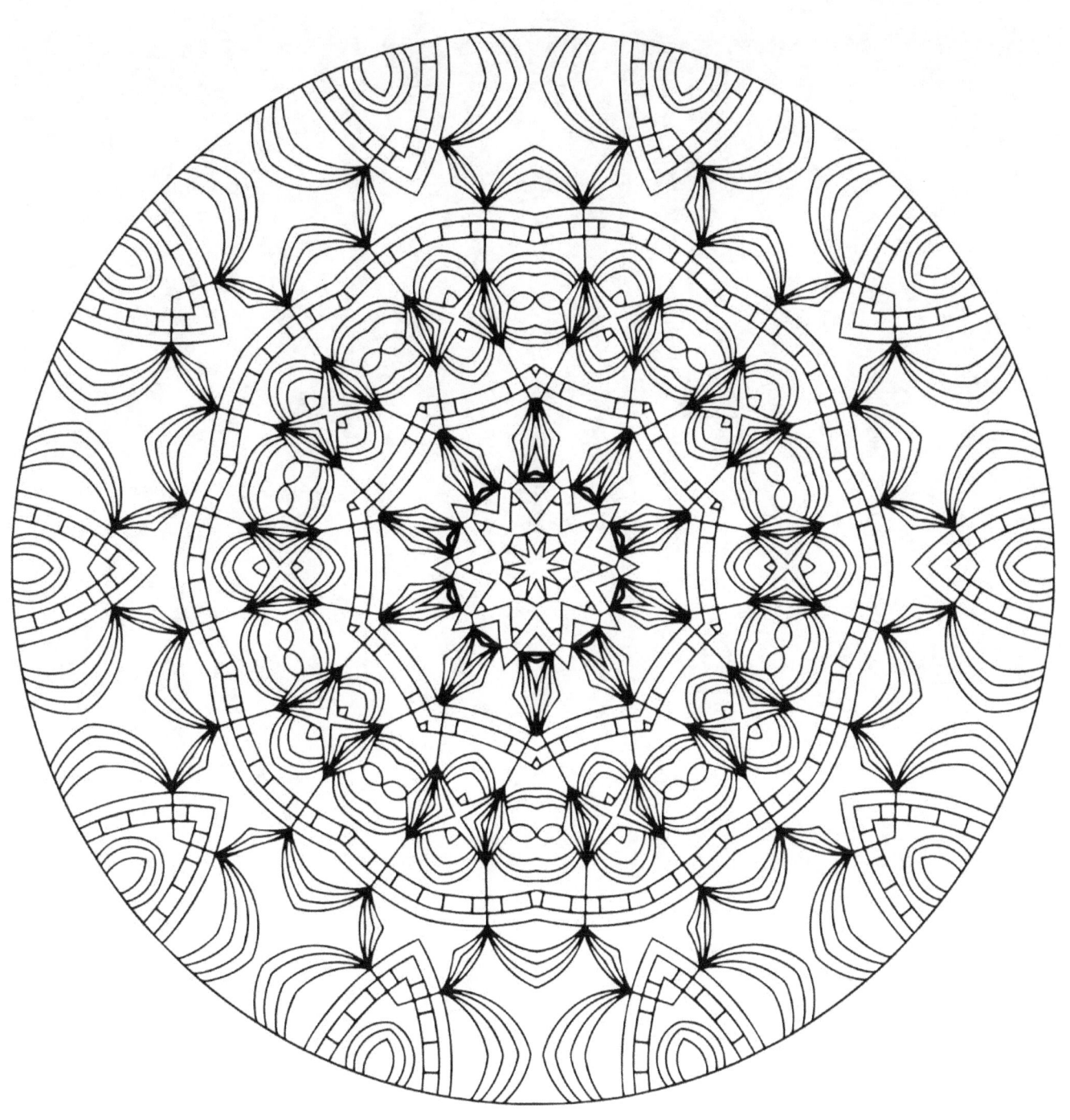

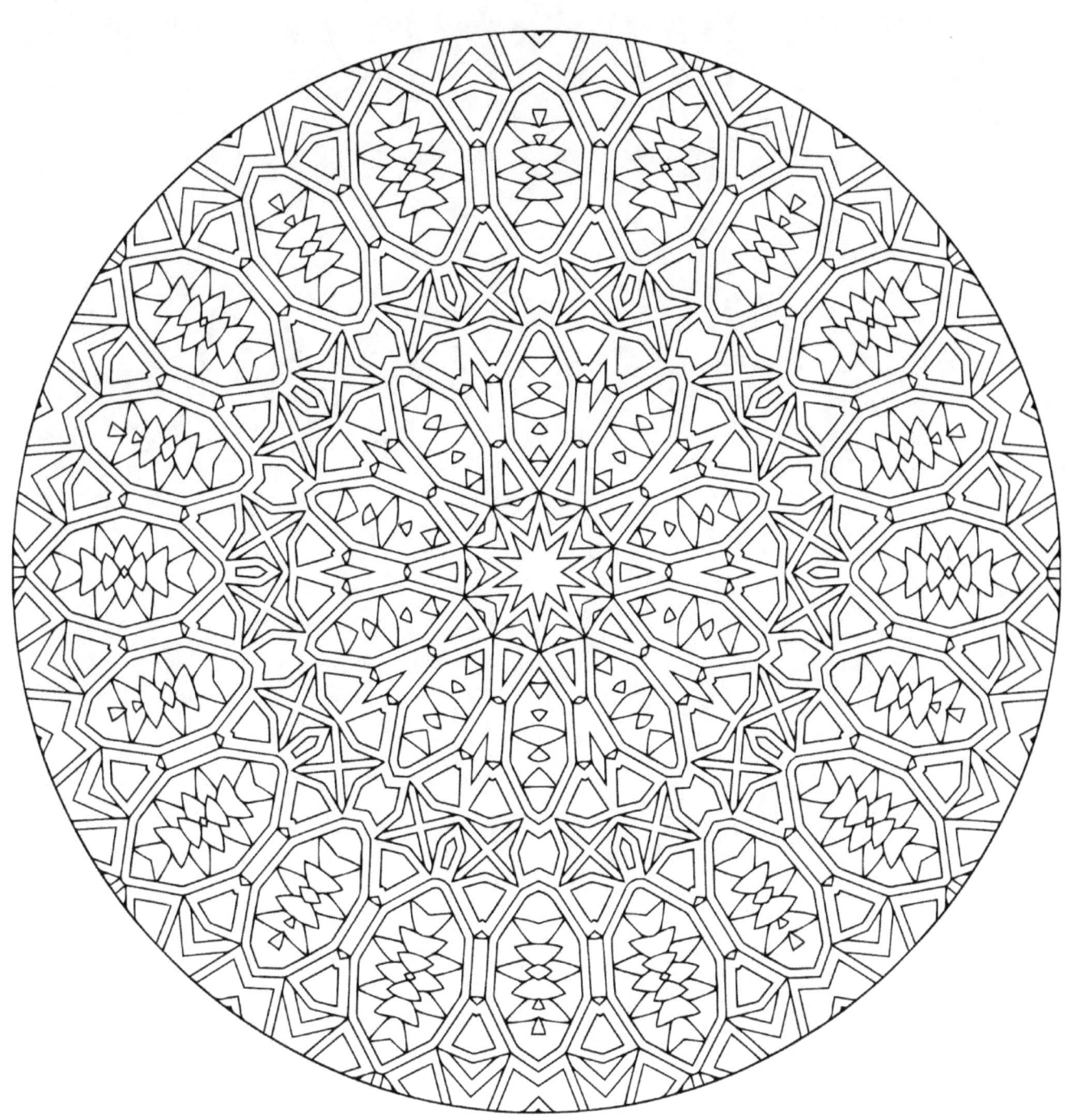

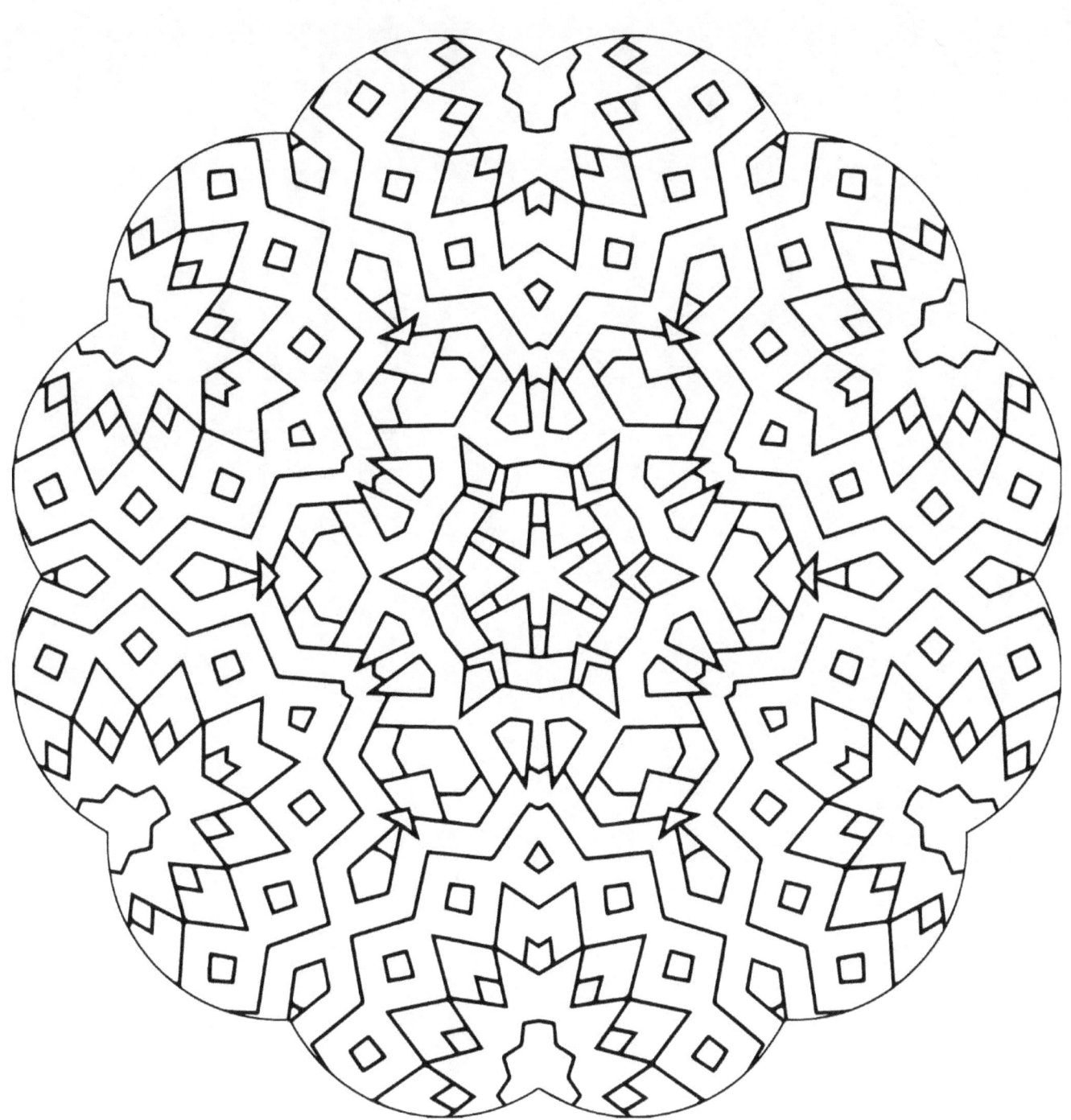

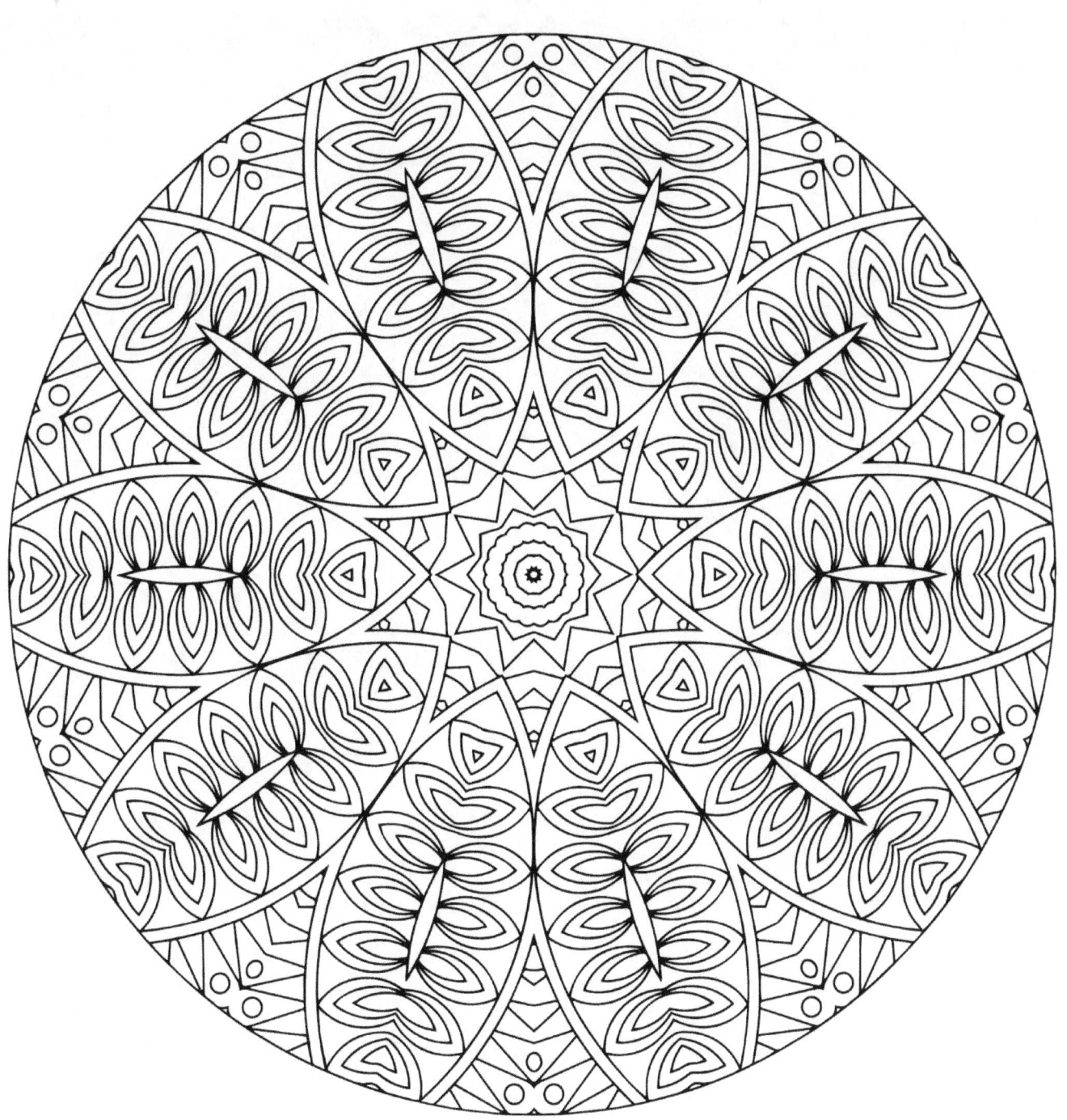

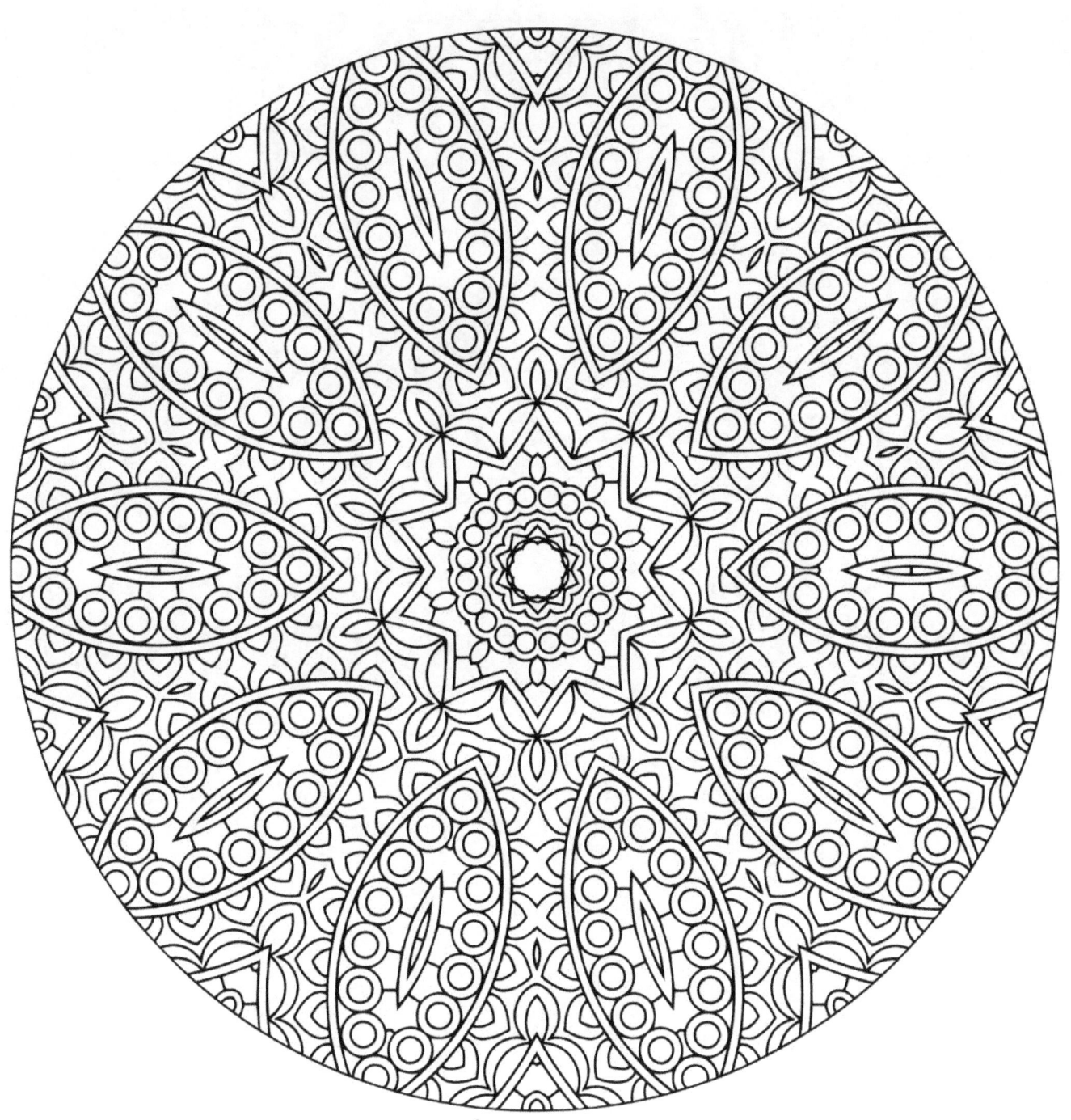

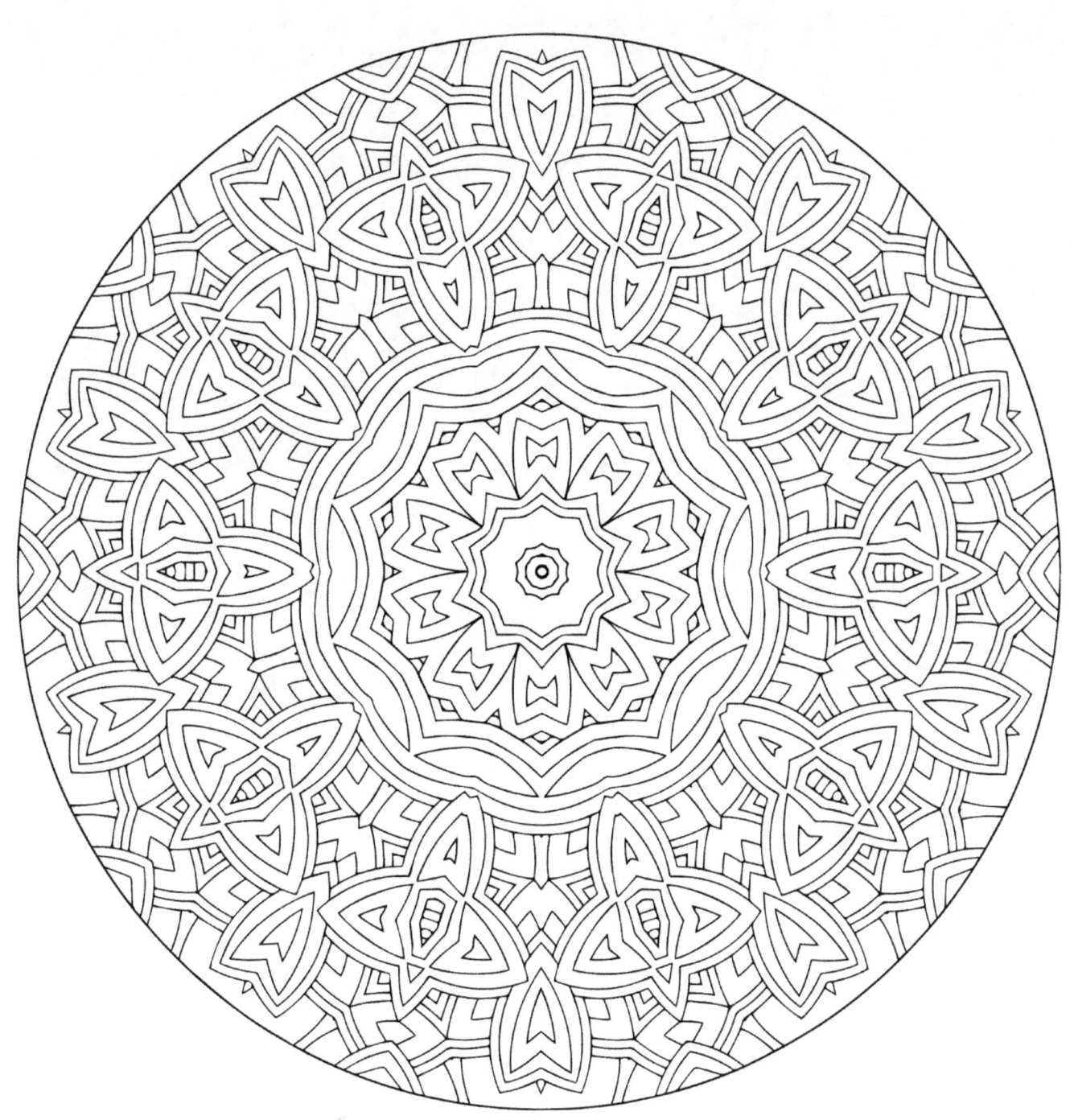

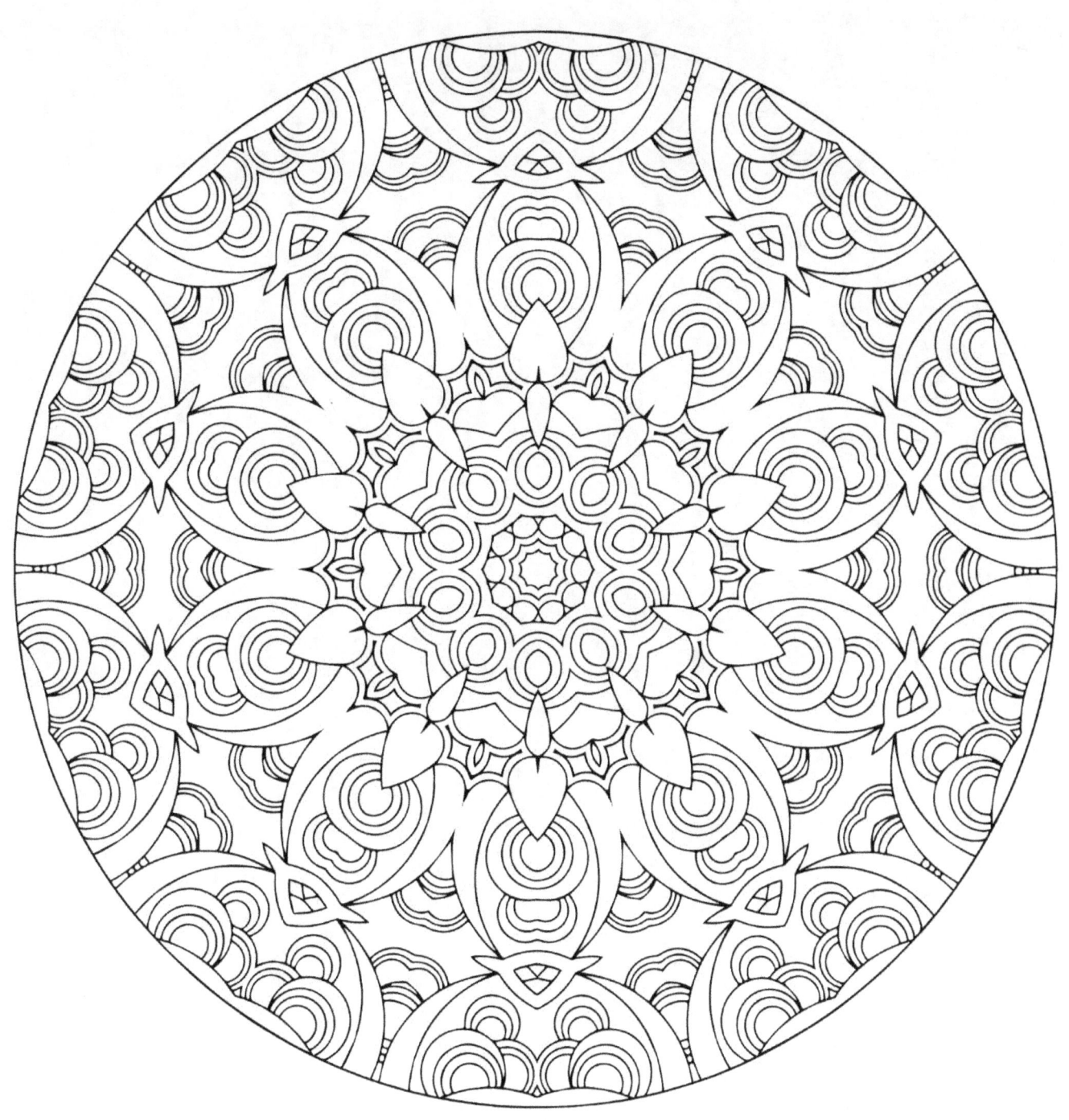

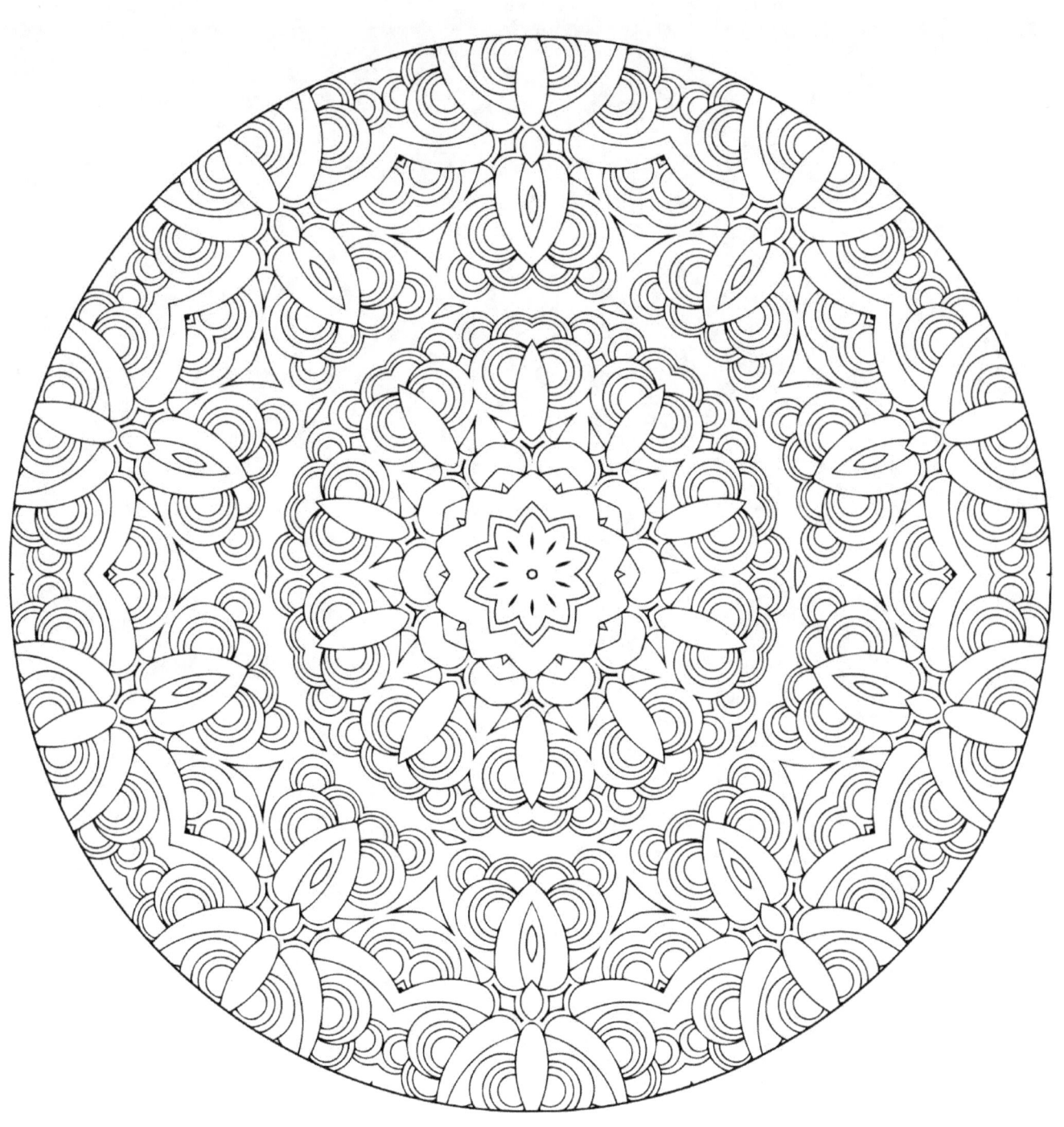

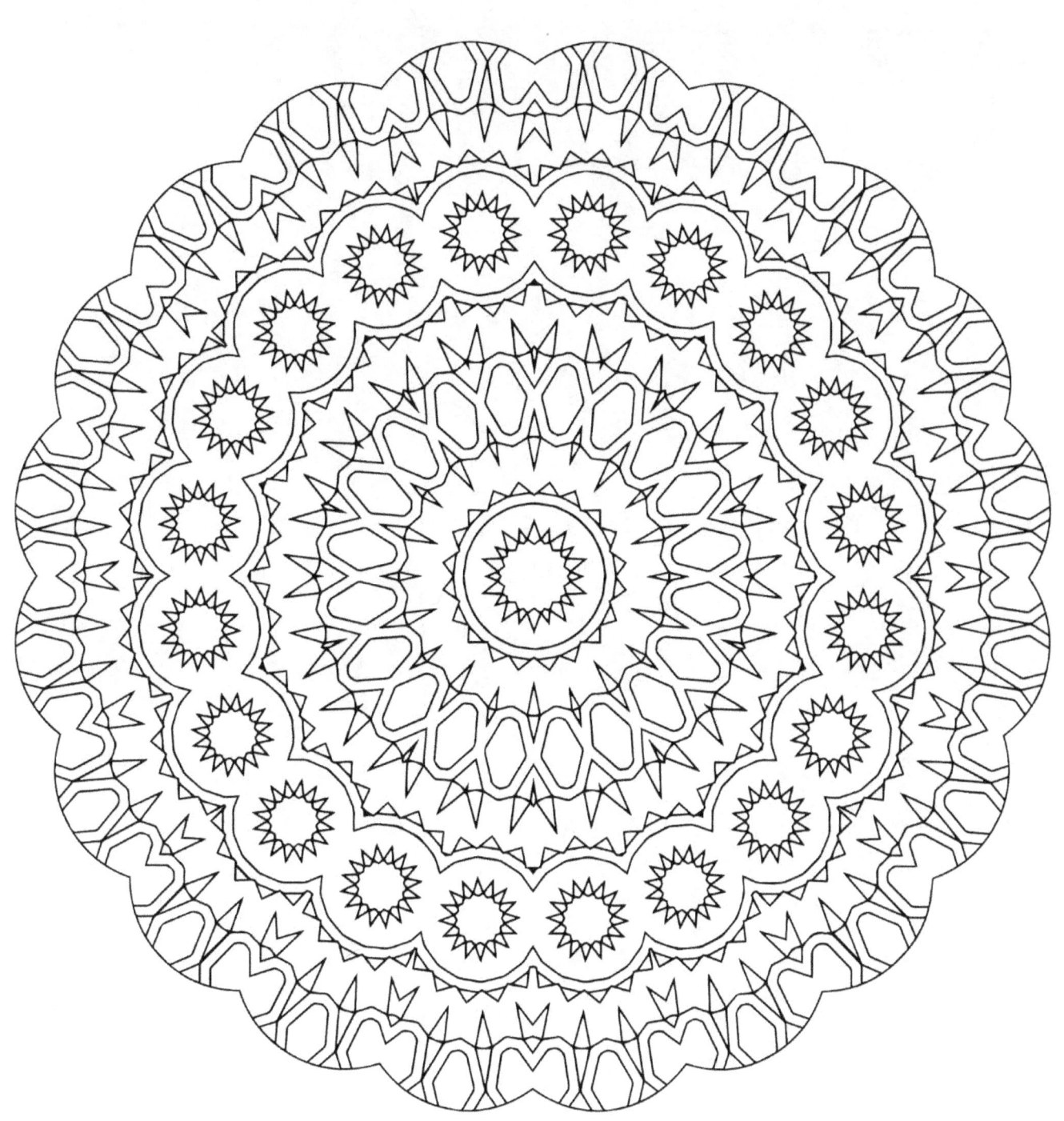

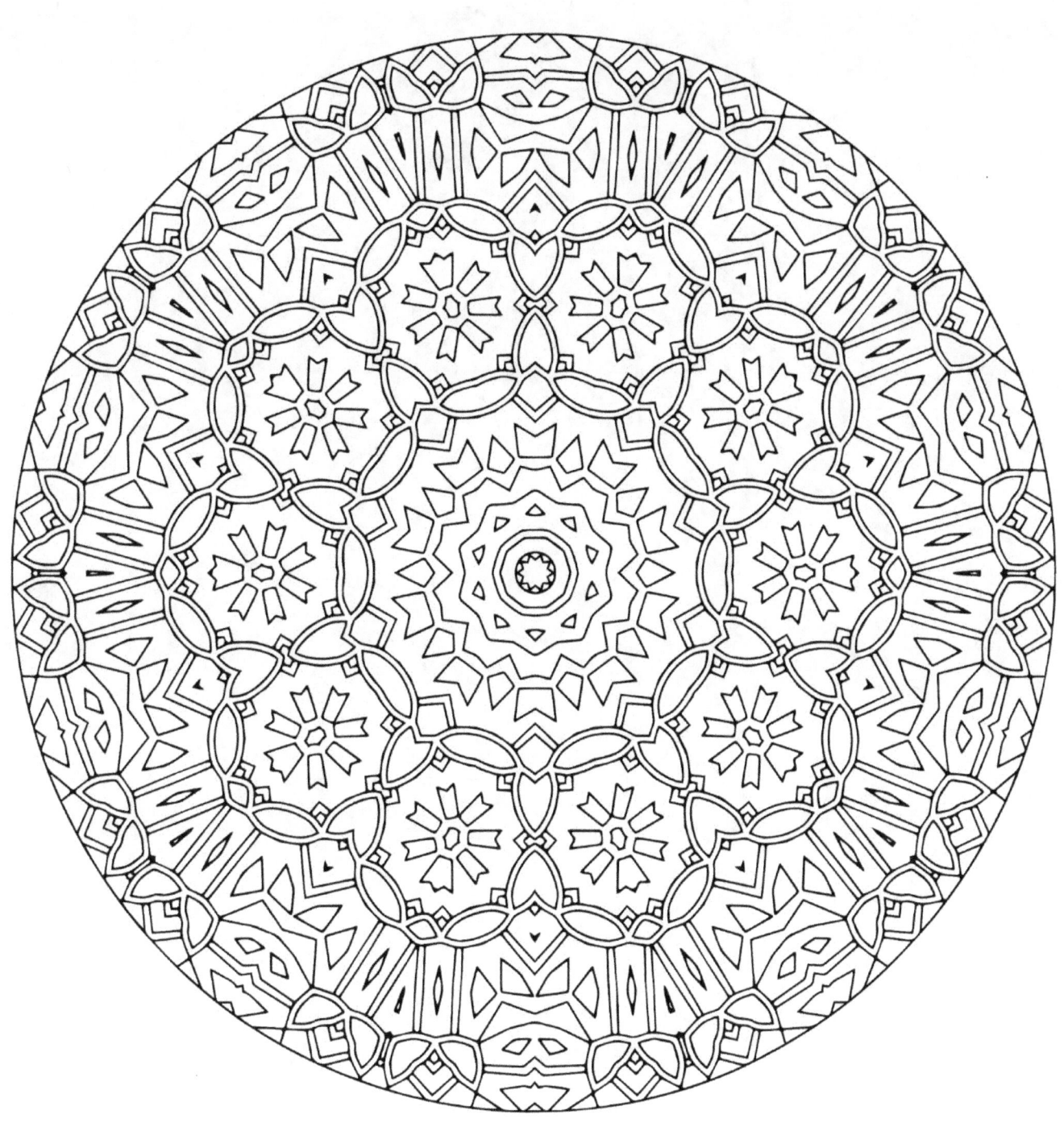

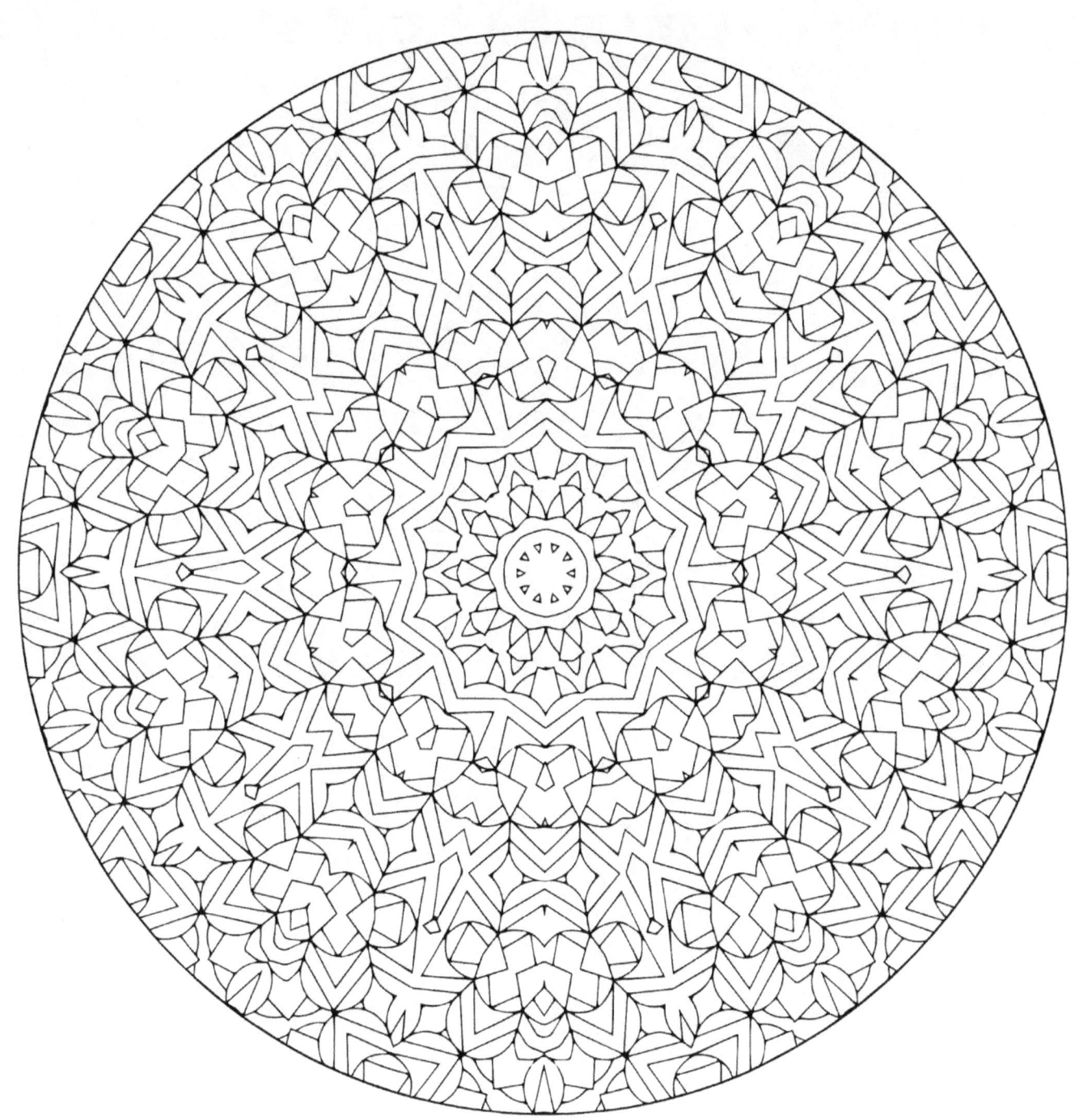

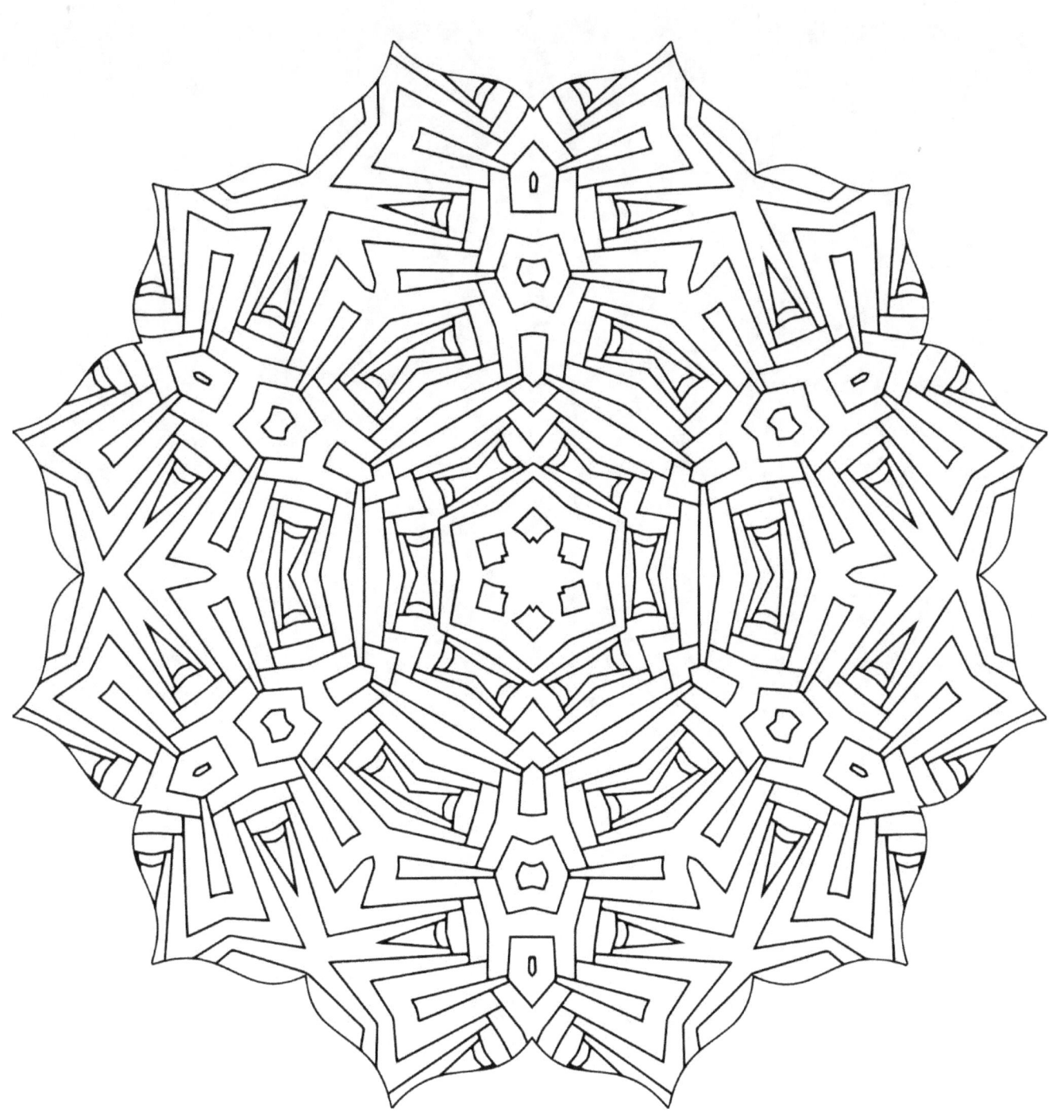

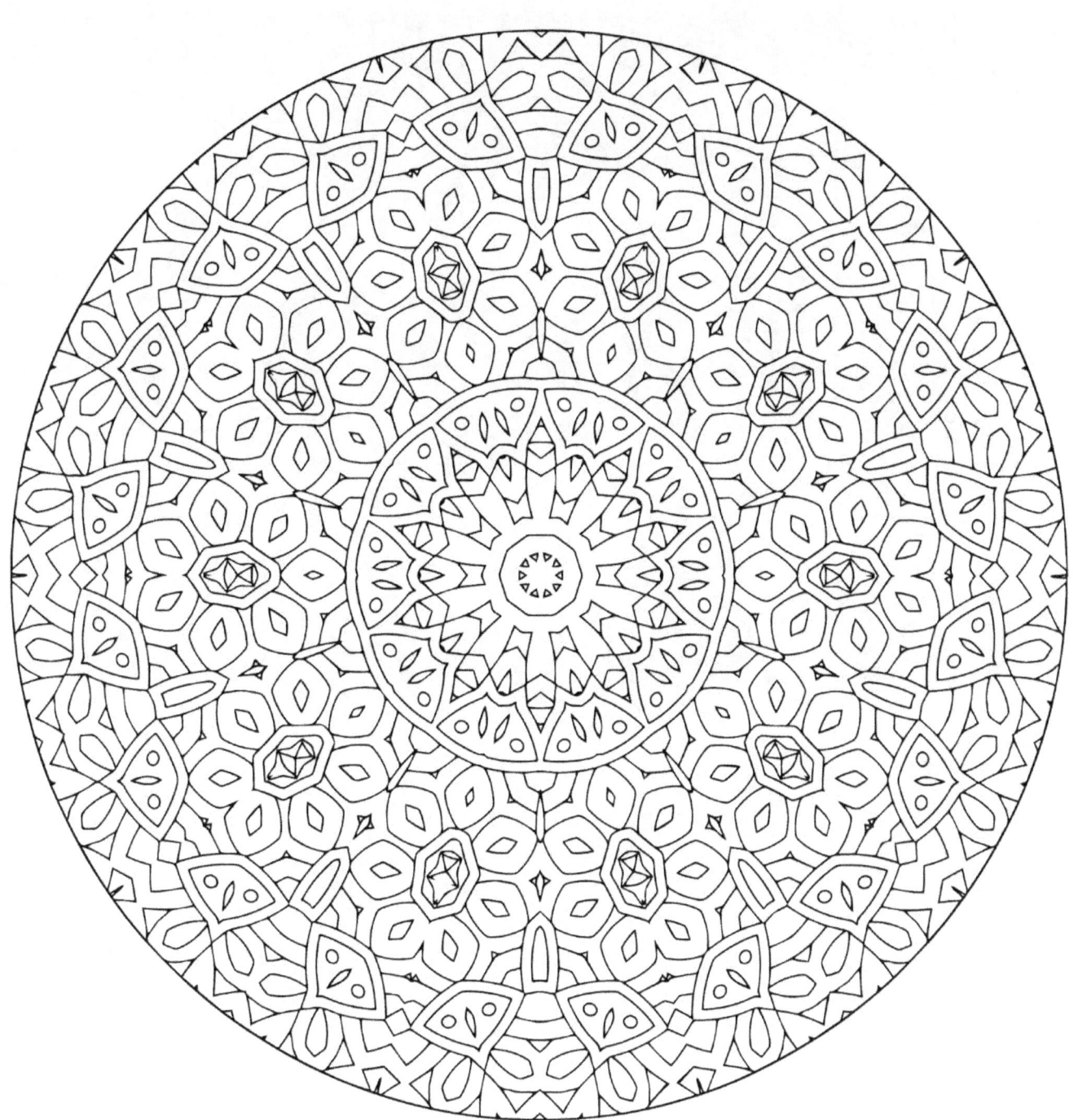

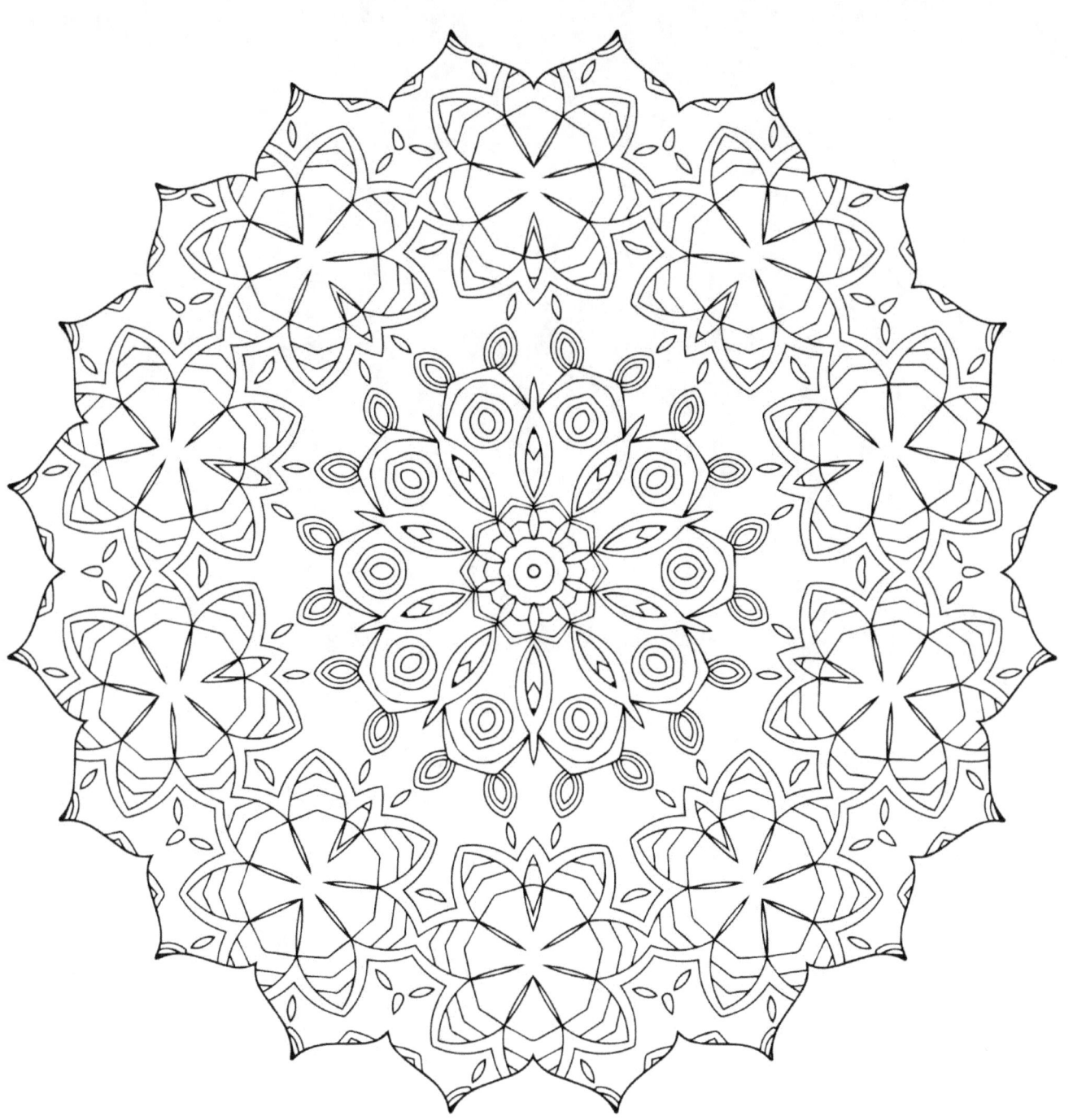

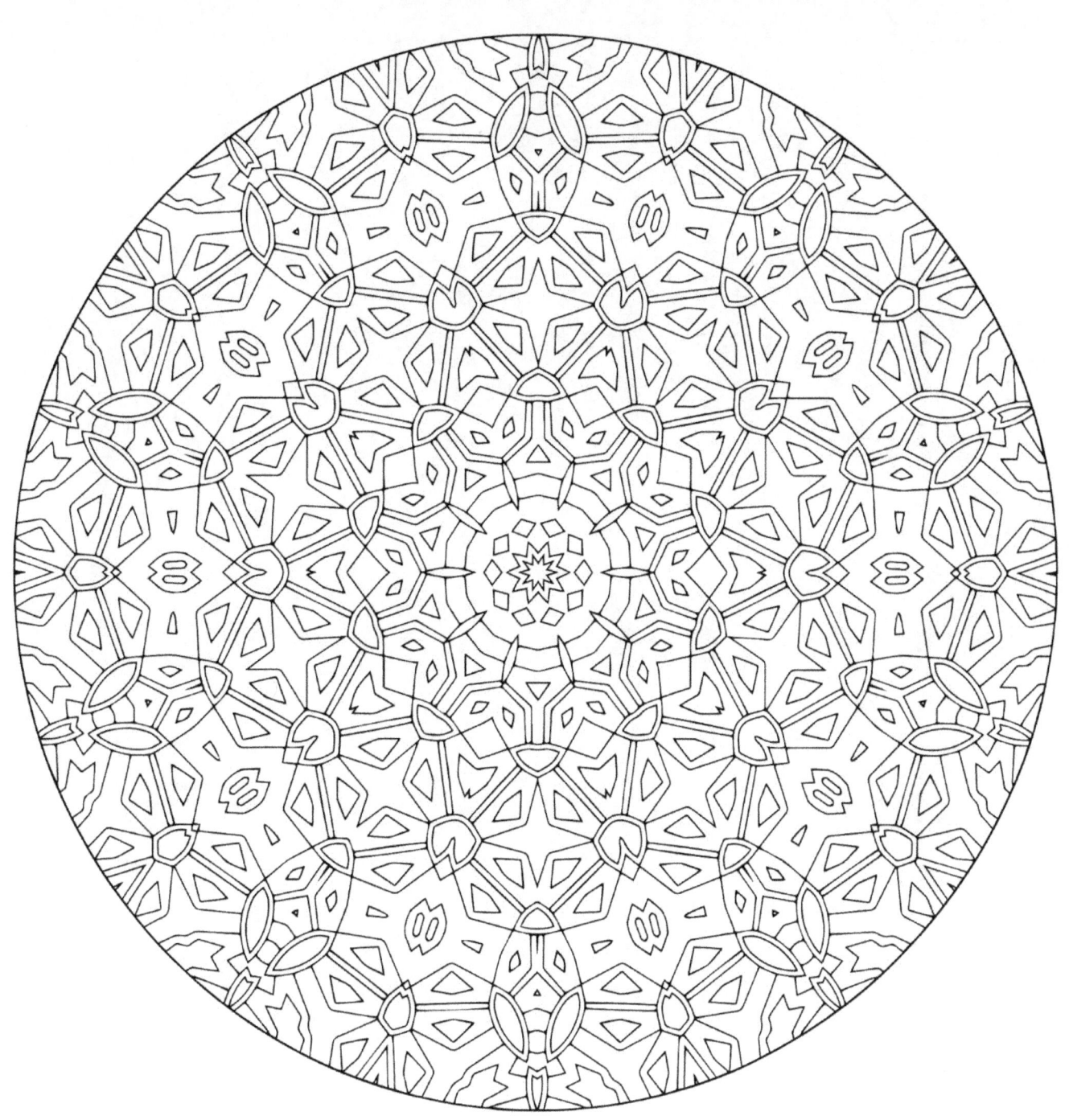

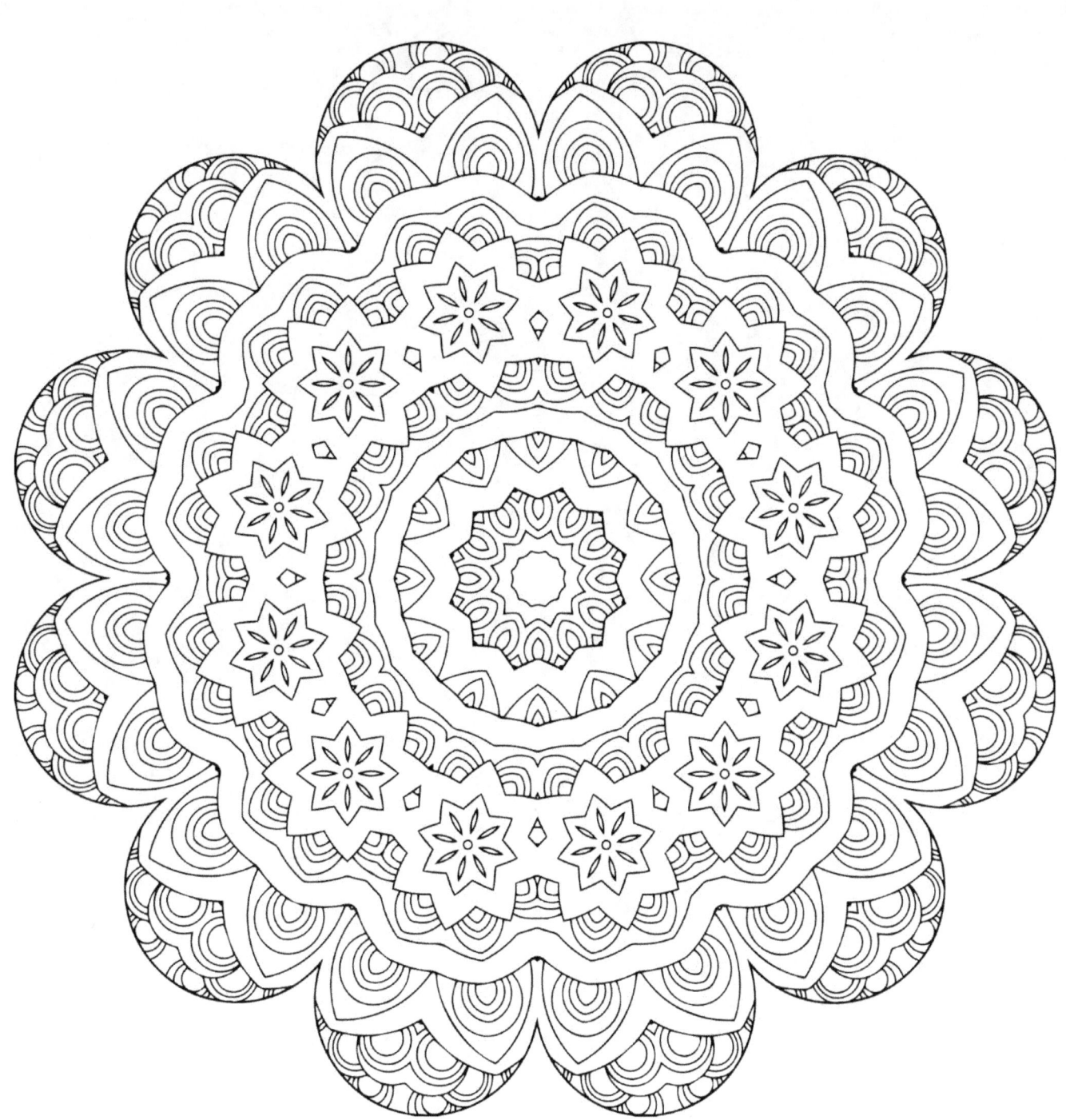

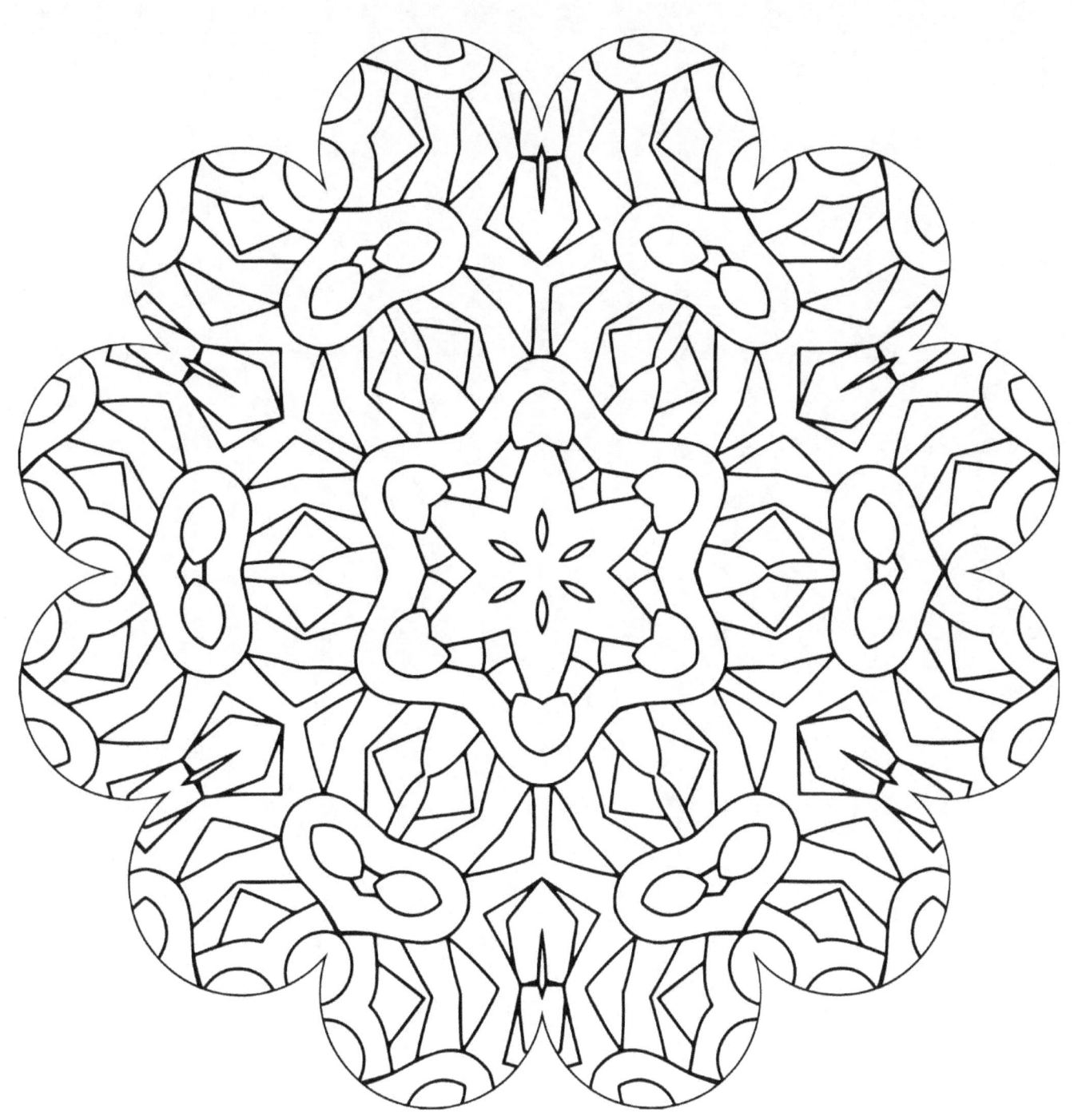

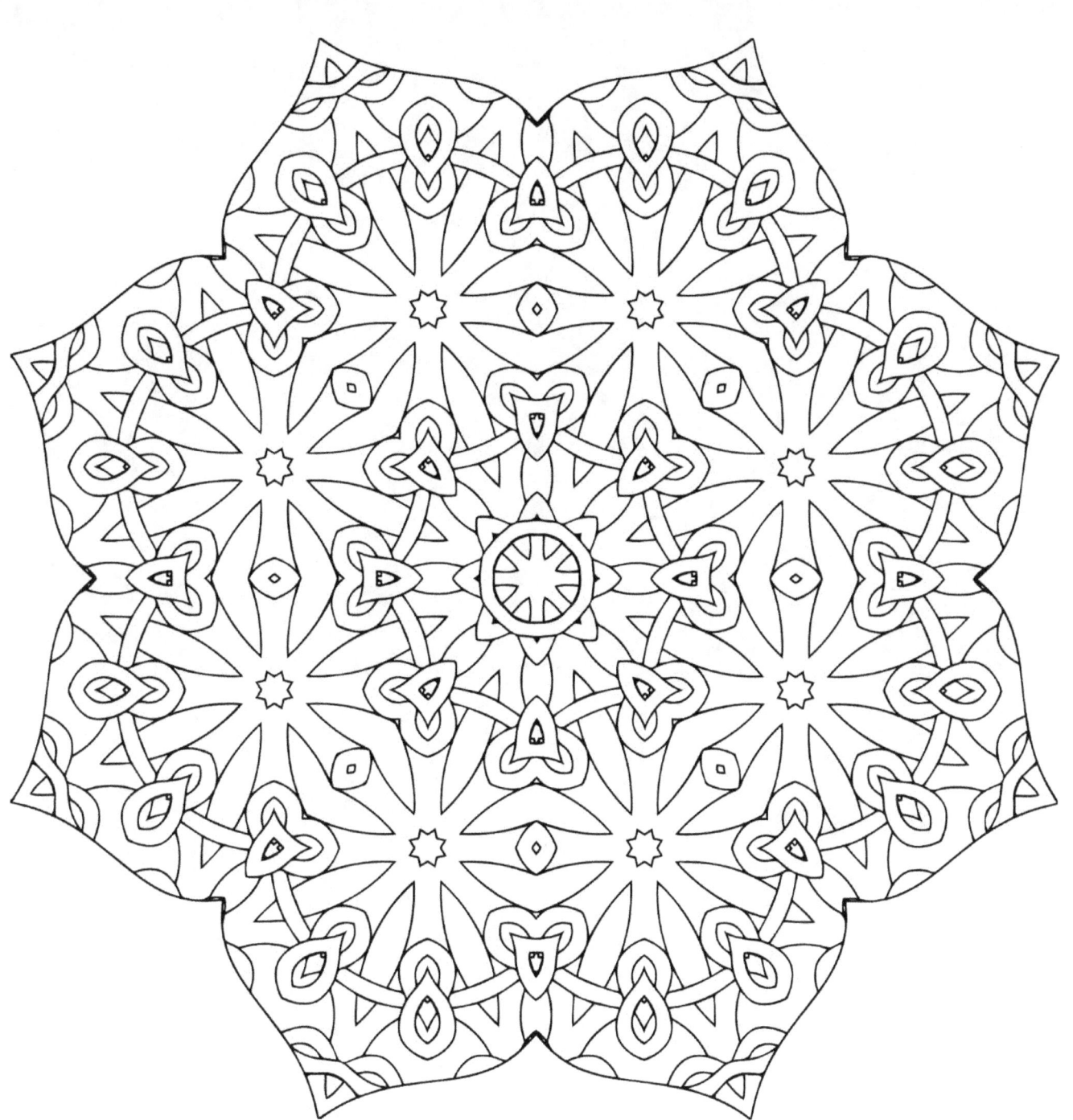

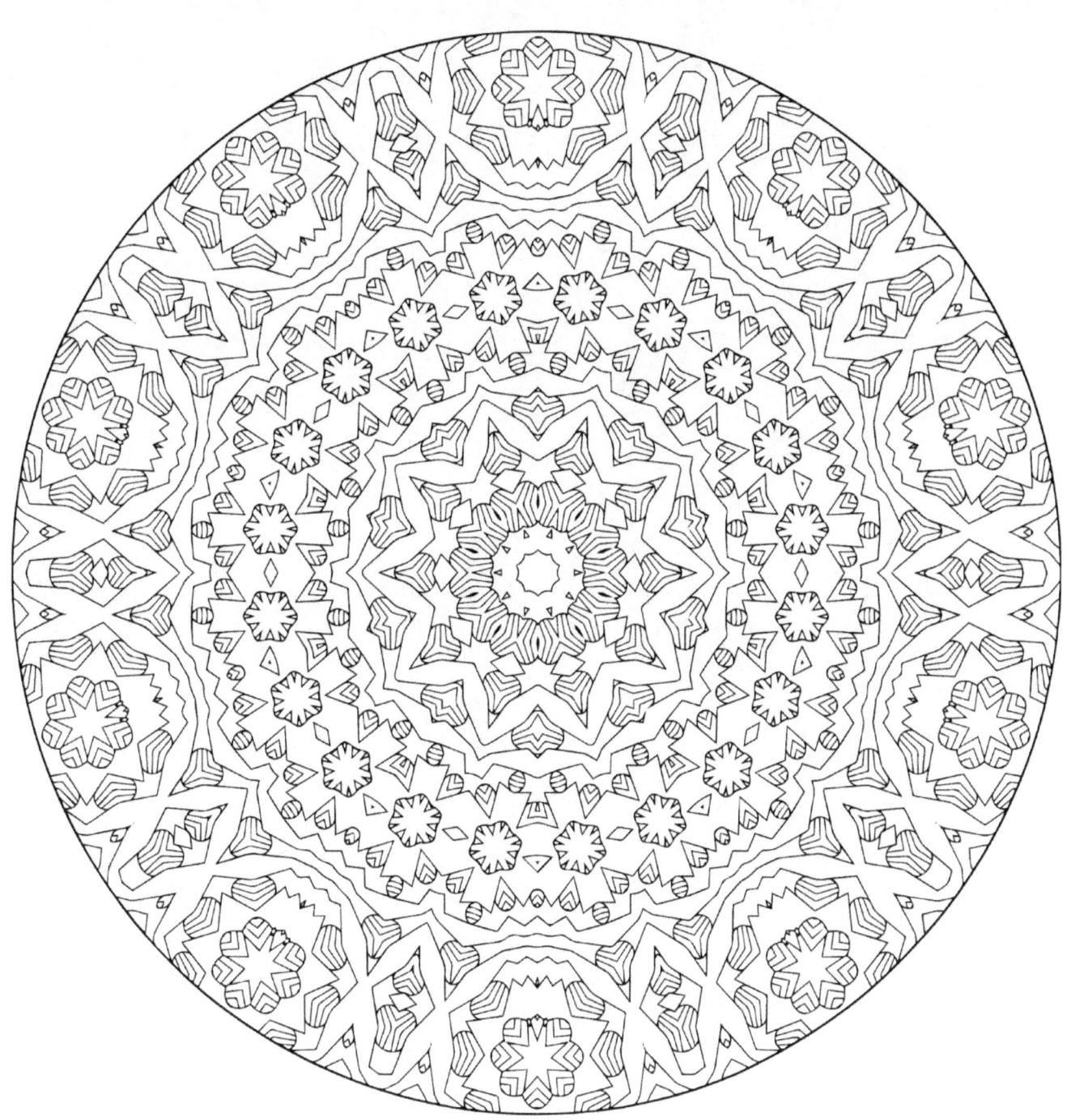

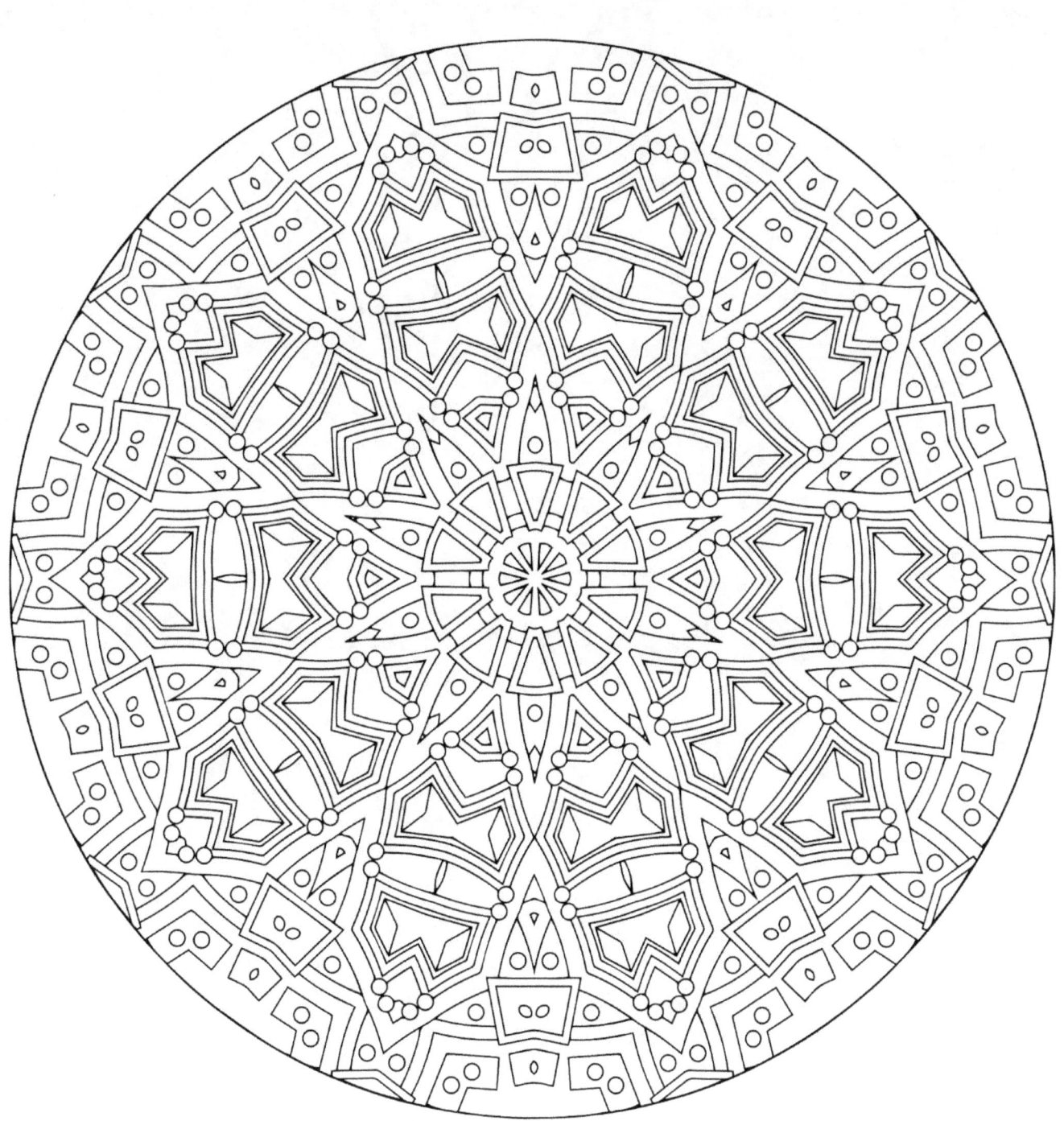

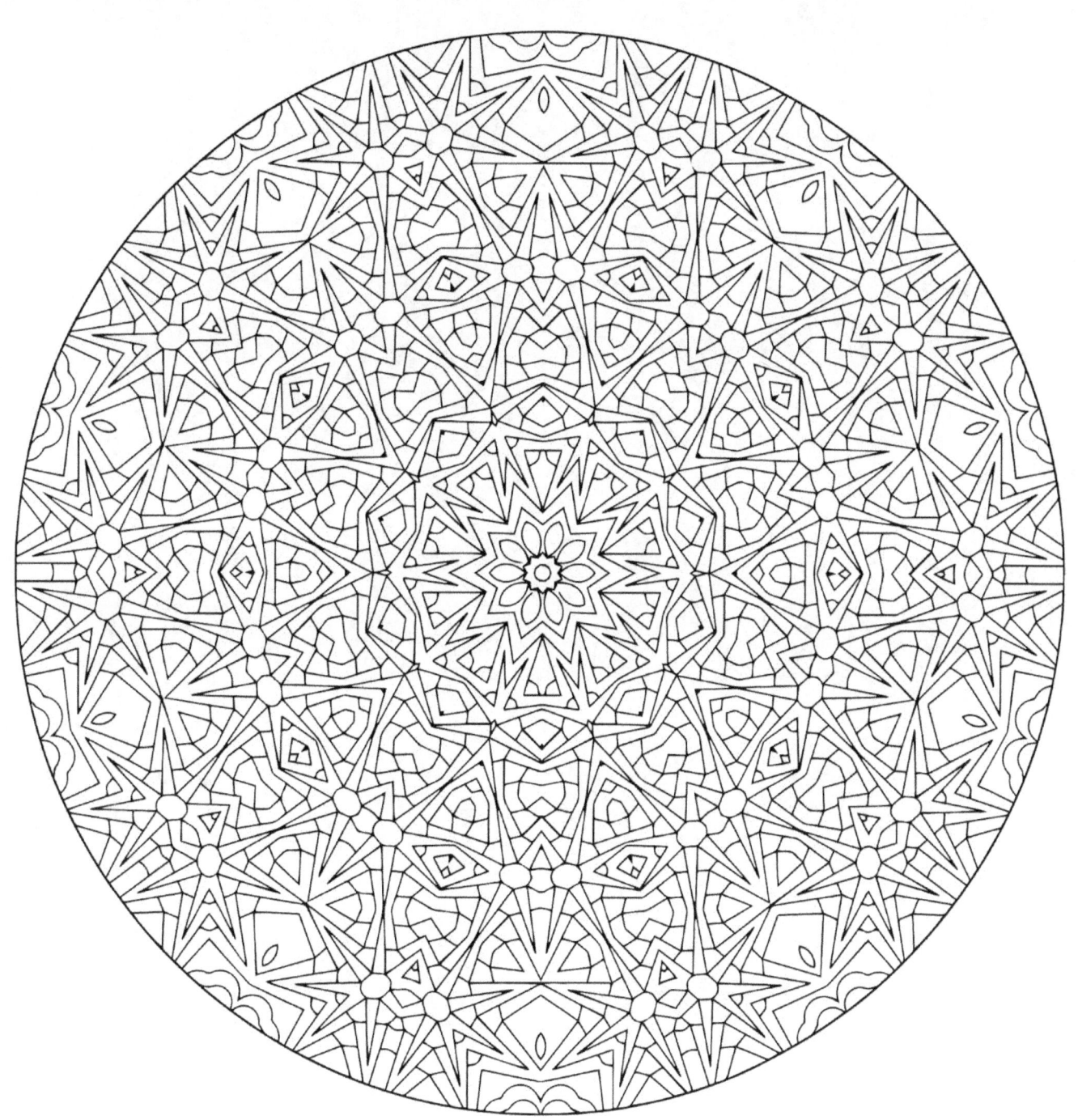

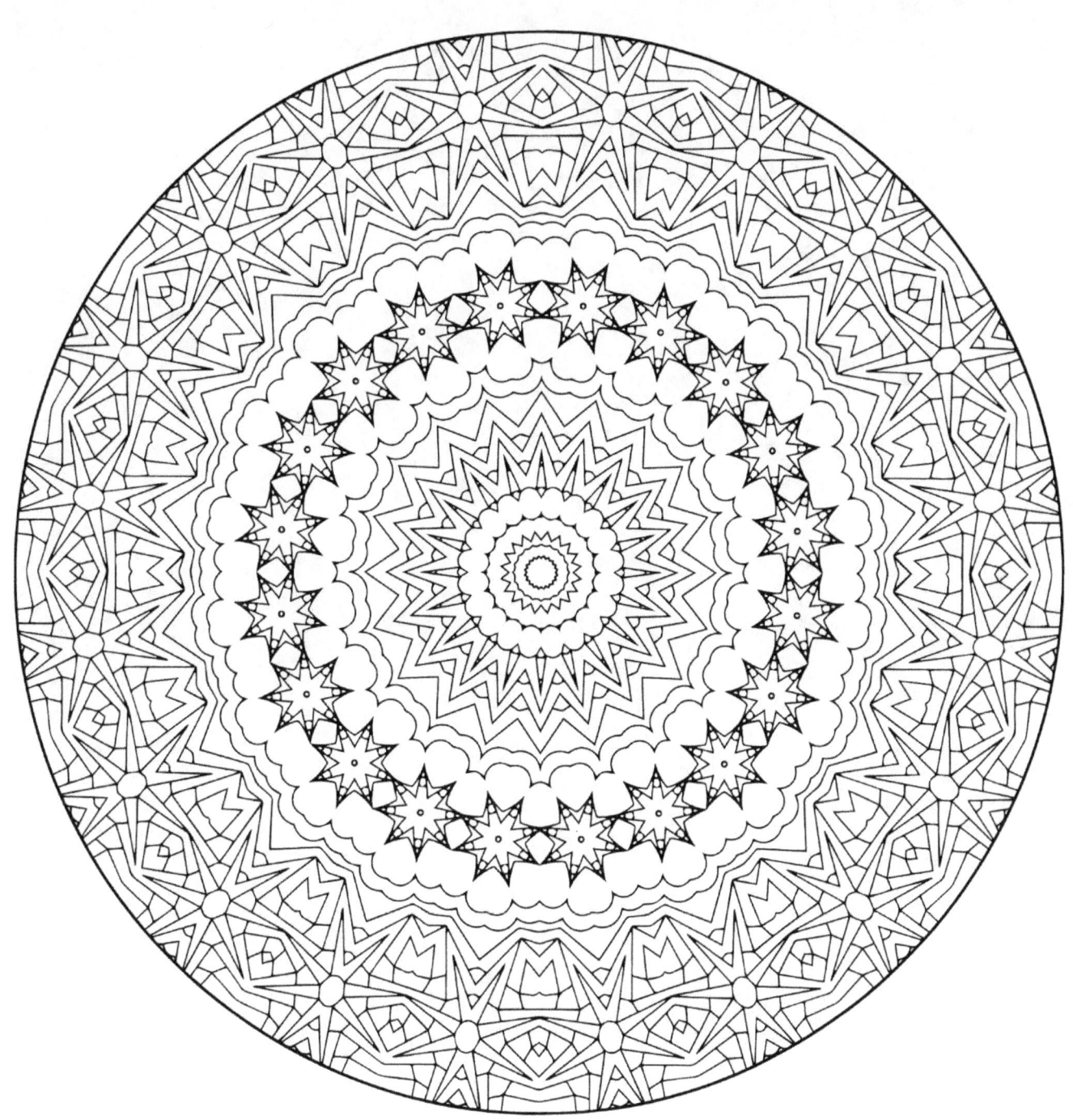

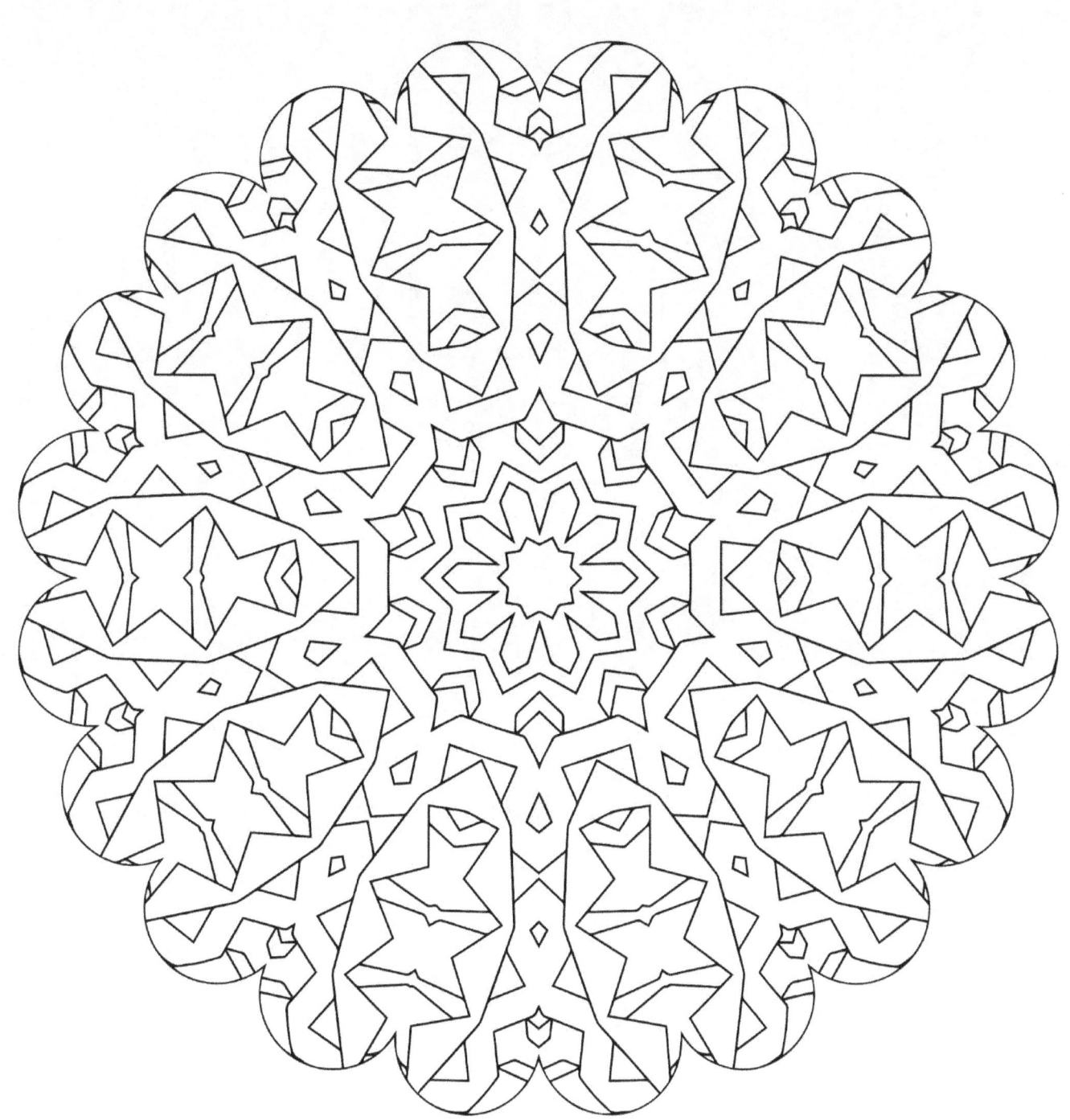

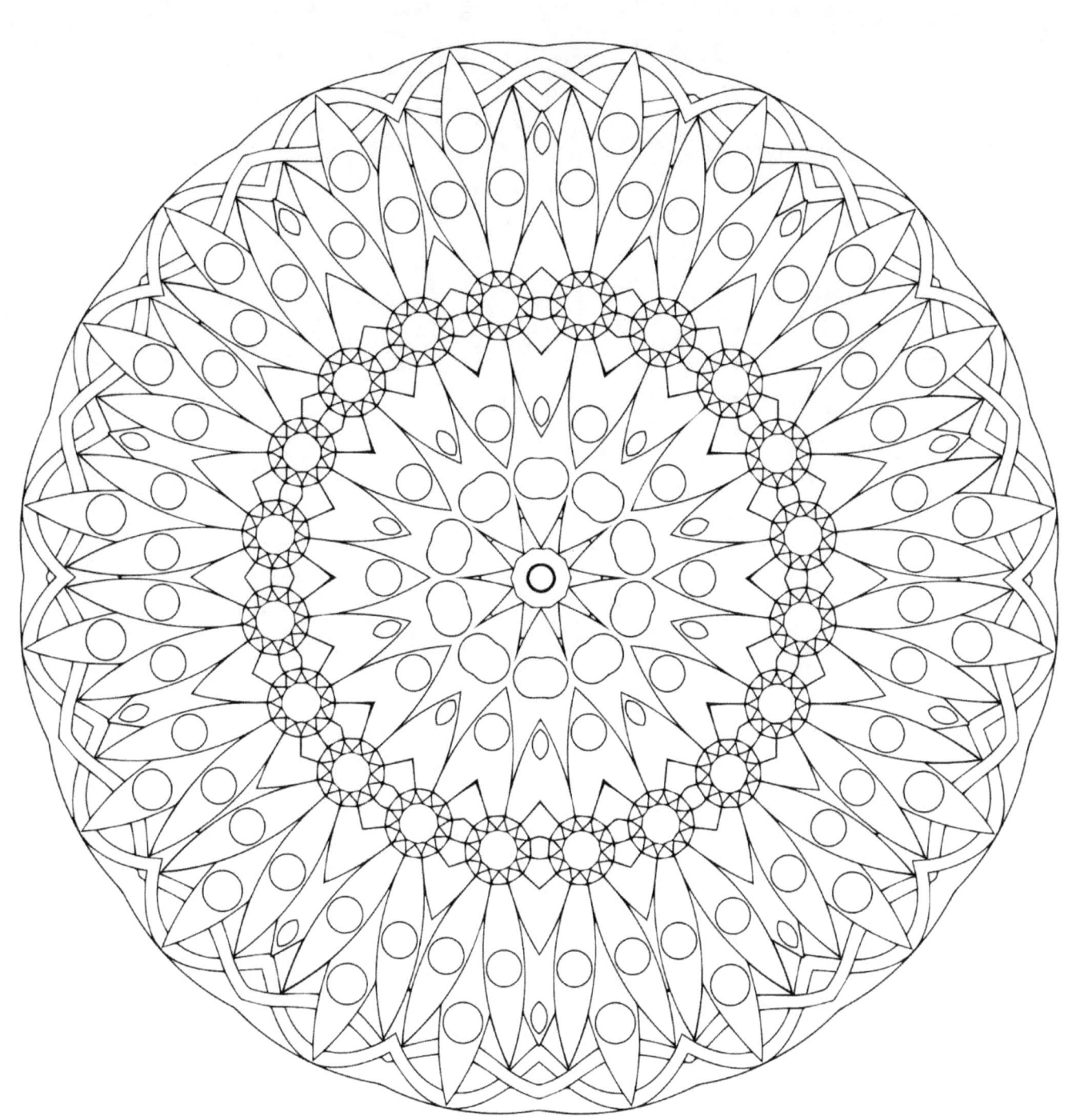

If you want to find out more about **True Coloring** and the other fabulous coloring books we have in store for you, then check us out:

Newsletter: Sign up for the **True Coloring** newsletter and get free coloring pages, plus notifications on all new releases: http://eepurl.com/b2rpc1

Pinterest: https://www.pinterest.com/**truecoloring**

Twitter: https://twitter.com/**TrueColoring**

Website: Truecoloring.com

Facebook Page: https://www.facebook.com/**TrueColoring**/

Instagram: https://www.instagram.com/**truecoloring**books/

Or

You may contact me directly at:

sharidaniel.coloringbooks@gmail.com

Or

https://www.facebook.com/profile.php?id=100011759205574